Between Words & Space

A collection of poetry and prose

Péjú Oshin

Published by Bakanna Books

Between Space & Words © 2021 by Péjú Oshin.

www.pejuoshin.com
www.bakannabooks.com

First published in 2021

ISBN 978-1-8384656-0-5

A catalogue record of this book is available from the British Library.

First printed in the United Kingdom

For the fleeting thoughts that never quite escaped our mouths during conversations that felt like they might hurt, the ones that appear at night when sleep refuses us space for recovery and the daydreams that ended abruptly.

Acknowledgements

Thank you to my ancestors, Mother, Father and siblings, Enam Gbewonyo, Lisa Anderson, Liz Gre, Gaylene Gould, Adelaide Damoah, Dawn. E, Caroline Hussey-Bain, Aisha Richards, Ade 'Àsìkò' Okelarin, J. Olayinka Ojo, Victor Ehikhamenor and many more whose names are in my heart and on my mind. Without your care, support, laughter, words of wisdom and encouragement this book wouldn't have been possible.

Thank you to the strangers on the internet who provided a safe space and encouraged and inspired me to read my poetry out aloud during a year that asked (forced) us all to re-examine how we show up in the world.

Finally, a huge thank you to the magic of Black women globally, unknowingly many of you have become mentors, aunties and sisters from a distance. Your thoughts and stories have nourished me, it is not only my hope, but a prayer too in that we are collectively restored.

Contents Page

It Begins

A Letter for the journey I never took   13
Travellers Cheques   14
Have You Eaten?   15
Puzzle Pieces   16
Finding Forever   17
The Cost of Laughter   18
Looking for Black joy   19
It Is but In A Name   20
Guidance   21
Limbo   22
Home   23
Bámi Gbé Omi (bring me water)   24
Elder Talk   27
Role Reversal   30
Forgive Me   31
Our Ancestors Died Multiple Deaths   32
Forget Me   34
Right Now   35
Still.In.Bed   36
A Letter for the Future   39

Value's Lost

A Letter for the Undervalued   43
Black Woman   44
Civility   47
Take Me Whole   48
For MJ   50
Concrete Tears   51
An Avoidance of Pain   53
Shipping   56

Waiting to Exhale   58
Relationship Glitch   59
Non-descript   62
Twisted Fantasies   64
Pit   65
Imagined Realities   66
The Stranger Is Easy   68
Stop Soothing   69
Conditions   70
Prayer   72
Be Still   74
A Letter for the lost   75

Desired Freedom

A Letter for Desire (Never Met)   79
All Praise To You   80
Becoming   83
Classroom et al   87
Touching Thoughts   88
Certainly Warm   90
Observer   93
Loving Black   94
Rainbows   95
The Winds   96
Between   99
Into the Night Sky   103
Building   106
A Thought for Grace   107
The Moment is Now   108
A Letter for seekers of Freedom   109

It

Begins

departure

give life

kin

movement

home

exist

care

disappointment

longing

burden

A Letter for the journey I never took

Dear Land,

Why is it so, that I meet you so firmly and
long to touch a sky that surrounds me, yet
escapes me?

I long for the gentleness of what I imagine,
would be your touch. The sands of the shore,
better yet, the soil that yields the crops we
feed on.

As I am far away, the only thing that now
comforts me is the hope that we might one
day again meet as you are my beginning
as well as my

end.

Travellers Cheques

Mixed feelings as you tell me of the
complexities surrounding the journey you
travelled to bring me here.

The excitement of youth
you set up a new life abroad and brought me
into the world.

The weariness attached to travel
determined to adapt to your new
surroundings
the inevitable embarrassment felt when life
was harder than you had expected.

All of this and all of us with an expectant
audience back *home*
who await the calls from the £5 phone cards
that finished within the blink of an eye
and left us wanting more

     you have one minute remaining

please send some money home

     the streets are not paved with gold

but how do you begin to speak to this?

Have You Eaten?

A journey to understanding you, we have
come from two different worlds,
the question is

    have you eaten?

The tears cried when you disciplined us,
your expectations were different from those
on the other side of the front door,
never a sorry for the confusion we felt,
simply just

    have you eaten?

The quiet of the house as the treatment of
silence is
enacted, no breaking of the ice,
you ask me once again

    have you eaten?

Language fails you
language has failed me.

Now we sit together
eating in a silence that is louder
than our thoughts.

Puzzle Pieces

Just another piece
          in a box pulled out only when the
world moves at a snails pace,
only on the rainy days.

I am reminded to look deeply at the ways in
which I show up here and the way I show up
there.

Here I am

          like a puzzle piece but one that does
not fit.

Home from Home
          on each continent sits a 'me' shaped
hole
          two puzzles that need me. On first
glance I seem to not fit, not by size or
          according to hue but it is the
          apprehension of fitting in where I
was never felt.

Finding Forever

Finding your place.
Finding your function.

The placement of one life into the context
of another and the infinite possibilities that
may emerge from this new formation
           but in this search is the drowning
and
suppression of life and spirit due to the
self-centered nature of another that
positions one life as
           better than the other.

Tell me of all the discomfort you feel in
witnessing the seismic shifts in traditional
culture and values.

Tell me of the initial uproar that was felt
and exhibited as a form of protest because
all that was natural, all that was normal has
now changed.

What did you leave behind?
Who really cares?

I'm forever finding because it was never
theirs.

The Cost of Laughter

Vulnerable as you are
this connection is twofold
subject to
subject you are
subject too.

Exposed you are magnified
deemed worthy of ridicule
judged.

You try to calculate
a measure of safety
let out, boxed in
reshaping the vulnerable
what do you find joy in?

Collectively we lament
in the name of death
happiness as our best kept secret.

Looking for Black Joy

Black joy
in the face of adversity
you reinvent yourself
time after time
you absorb light
you are light
emanating warmth
emanating excellence
for too long it seems
the world has tried
taking away joy
that which is Black.

No more, today is yours
tomorrow is promised
Black joy

here you are.

It Is But In A Name

You called for Black joy,
Ayo
she, he, they
custodian of a name
that speaks into existence
your very being.

You are loved
praised you are
called to.

In foreign lands
they call not to you
through you
but over and around you.

The unknowing place
little value in your name
bearer of dreams
yet to be dreamt
a force for change
yet to be met
a call to wealth
a richness, harboured in you.

Guidance

Speak to me,
so that I might know the direction
the wind takes me in
as I look to the night sky
wondering where I may land next.

A hand on my shoulder,
the softness of your calling,
I yearn for the wisdom of your life
and those passed.

The melting frameworks,
stories untold,
a generation apart
but a love between,
I search across,
up and then down
for where our stories should
and might intersect.

A lineage of hope,
the brave knows no bounds,
walk with me.

Limbo

I am in limbo, the liminal for my tongue is
tied between a language that I understand
but fail to speak.
The trapped thoughts that travel from my
brain to die a watery death in my
oesophagus, maybe smothered by the
combination of pounded yam and ogbono
soup, words that were never to meet the air
of the day.
Those words stay stale as my mouth betrays
me, the speech they expected me to speak,
the tongue of my mother is that which
chokes me now.
I watch in silence like a thief, waiting for
any opportunity to create sound, the rawkus
laughter, a disapproving haa, a gentle mmm,
anything to let them know that although
I cannot speak, I am one of them and they
have been heard by the one who resembles
them and so is familiar yet unknown.

Home

Home is…

Wherever you are, except for the fact that you are nowhere to be found.

Home is…

The sound of your voice when I close my eyes, but recently it has been like the static of grandpa's radio as I switched between the channels

I can't hear
you.

Home is…

The safety of your hug, but I am no longer small enough to be cradled in your arms as I sit on your lap, because the weight of I and my problems may break you.

It broke
me.

Home is…

I'm still trying to figure out where home is.

Bámi gbé omi (bring me water)

It is through tradition that I root myself in a
land that I may have never visited apart from
in my dreams
but one that no less belongs to me and so
becomes one that I am urged to protect and
maybe serve.
I am a custodian, maybe even a farmer.
You ask me to bring you water, that which
I use to cultivate all that anchors me to the
soil of my father, the soil of my mother.

Our soil.

      My soil.

I take my role as custodian with a
seriousness that is wrapped in warmth
because as a child, I was set a task which
seemed to be for me and me alone. One that
externalised my childish glee, sitting in the
company of friends who became family, the
extended network of kin in lieu of blood,
this community here is all I need.

"Bámi gbé omi"

This task is for you.

On your tiptoes, you reach for the silver of
the tap, your head bobs over the rim of the
sink. It is stiff but you persist. With
anticipation you try as your task is yet to be
complete, the tap complies and now you're
mesmerised by the stream that emerges from
the faucet.

"Omi da?"

You hear it from a distance
and so you fill a bowl
almost to the brim
cradling it like the baby you still are.

To the living room I go with expectant
guests, a towel over my tiny arm. Each
person washes their hands and with a shake
and a pat dry they prepare to eat.

They wash the sins of the day off their hands
and their hearts, in the company of the ones
they love.

They roll their sleeves up for this is work.

To love and to live in commune is not an
easy task, to maintain those relationships,
is not an easy task. But here they are, lights
dimmed low and the chatter of subjects that
didn't quite make sense to me in my childish
form.

Time passes.

You are my faucet, my community.

A stream of love, nourishment, counsel,
discipline, joy and laughter - untapped and
unfiltered.

You asked me to bring you water, remember
that you are mine.

Elder Talk

Trapped in these four walls,
maybe she's to blame too.

The burden is too much.

Although she wished her luck,
it was clear that she was stuck
And she projected her loneliness onto her.

It was the little things,
like the way she would close the door,
the increasing volume of the spirituals she
hummed
all to let her know, that as Elder, she was
hurting,
that she wanted her attention, to spend time
with her.

That was the last thing she wanted to do.

She had spent her entire life trying to
connect with her.

It was the way Elder looked at her like she
was some kind of hero when in-fact it was
Elder who should have been her hero,
but she was not.

She felt increasingly disappointed by this
woman she had once looked up to because
with age she realised, there was nothing
about her,
nothing of which she saw within herself and
wanted to model,
but everything she hated about herself and
why she struggled in society was in the elder
who was supposed to have shown her the
way,
it's a struggle when this is all that you see.

With each day that goes by she feels
damaged.
She wants out, to get away from her because
Elder damages her,

she is damaged.

Elder imposes herself,
she is not present,
she is never listening,
she does not comprehend.

She absorbs Elder's tears,
her emotions,
her traumas.
                The burden is too much,
so she cuts ties.

That's what she needs,
to be away from the dysfunctional Elder
because everyone pretends that it's all ok
when, in-fact, it is not.

Elder knows better
but this must come to a stop.

Role Reversal

Baby
Mother

I was once the baby
but now I am the mother
to my mother
our roles reversed
with no warning.

I regret my desires past
a wish to grow fast
now here in adulthood
I crave for days simpler.

Nothing really mattered
I was only half responsible for me
and the other half,
for you.

Now I sit here,
teaching you the ways of the new world,
summoning patience from an inner being,
perhaps the patience you never fully afforded
me,
it hurts to give you this,
but I do so anyway.

Forgive Me

Forgive me child,
I love you, those words I couldn't say
A mouth full of rocks
For me, it was never the done way.

Forgive me child,
My outward expression is mute, but I'm
prouder than you'll ever know
Inu mi dun
I am smiling from within.

Forgive me child
As you've gotten older, I see the harm that I
have done,
I left it to a child to interpret my thoughts
Forgive me, for I am still a child too.

Our Ancestors Died Multiple Deaths

Dear ancestors

I have come to realise that
when you died
it was not but once
nor twice, but multiple times.

Your first death was slow
painful
witnessed by many
intervened in by none.

The next was quick
in a room full of witnesses
you drew your last breath
in the blink of an eye
you passed between
this world and the next.

As you made meaning
navigating a new terrain

your children
they remembered you
calling into the frequencies
willing you back into the physical.

The children
they too had children
with limited memories of you
now they grow up
they too navigate a new terrain
but your descendants do not cry for you.

Your first deaths seem not enough
subjected to the frivolous
spirit, disheartened
exhumed without cause
destined to float in between
the ancestors never sleep.

Forget Me

Forget me like your life depended on it,
Forget me like I forget myself
Forget me, no one ever seems to put me first.

Right Now

Where we are right now is a place of
discomfort that we did not dream of and one
that begged us to keep connected through a
line that was not straight and as such, met
with multiple interruptions.

A place that gave us no warning or
timeframe for how long we might dwell here
because right now is yesterday
and yesterday is

        tomorrow.

We wonder if we'll make tomorrow when
today has been the root cause of our undoing
and unknowing in truly believing whether or
not the place of right now

        is right.

Still. In. Bed.

Take me away with your dreams
that I may enter your thoughts at night
because the day is unkind and unaligned.

I feel like I'll never see you.

I prayed for the day we would reunite and I
might be held in your arms,
the safety that I craved,
the intimacy you waved in,
but then we

                    can't get enough.

I hear the winds rushing up against my
window to let me know it is willing to take
away my worries,
that I don't have to sit unsure in the
gardeners' club
remembering the pond that was built
to create an oasis in the city,
because the grey of the tower blocks is all we

ever knew.

The same few locations out of necessity and
survival
my horizons needed broadening,
a home away from the piss-soaked stairwells
and lifts,
the broken lights that led the blind to lead
the blind,

we didn't know any better,
we didn't have any better, but we tried
to transcend the fears that we inherited
from a world that was colder than we knew
possible.

Memories of a childhood without a care in
the world,
memories of something that didn't quite feel
right but stayed,

the unwanted guest who refused to make
their bed
left dirty dishes in the sink and washed your

dirty linens in public,

                              because who gives a
fuck?

Not you or I

but the sound of the bank deposit at the end
of each month reminding me that I
contribute to society
but that this is what you see my labour as

worth.

A Letter for the Future

Dear Future,

Between states of sleep and wake, I wonder
how and when you will reveal yourself and if
in some parallel
universe I am already here with you
because the stitch that

holds

the past and

now together is

already here

and

somehow

still stitching because the future is

now.

I'm learning to embrace the unknown and
about to break all signifiers of time so that I
might avoid the perils of debt and spend you
well.

Value's
Lost

worthy of

love   desirability

wisdom

loss

journey

hope/less

rebuild

A Letter for the Undervalued

Dear Value,

I must admit, you are a little unfair.

Well...maybe a lot.

You play a game that has no rules with players
who do not understand their parameters
because quite frankly, they are not real.

where do you lie?
        within or on the out?

Your worth is subject to fluctuation based on
a whim,
a play for power by the wicked who engage in
this as sport.

When will you tell the truth, that they might
know and one day be free?

Black Woman

Dear Black Woman,

Sorry for you, sorry for I,

The world washes you with its dirty lies and
expects you somehow to pretend it doesn't
smell.

Who deserves this, not you, not I, but
somehow the buck stops with us.
Expectant with no work,
hesitant with no worth

the world is cold and we just need a little
more, can we bask in the glow
of our spirits past,
be told that you're beautiful
without condition and
without limitation.

But for I,
you're ok for a Black girl,
even amongst us,
a raging criticism that tells us we always
measure short.

The tape isn't long enough
to record all my insecurities,
better still
all my star qualities.

Look up and you'll see me,
mother of the earth
without a perceived care in the world
bar the fact,
that I bare the weight of caring for the
world.

Where is value,
the value that they changed to make it so
that my own never matched that of yours
because the competition was rigged
so that we always participated
but never grabbed
that win.

Hold on, slow down, turn me inside out,
the mellowed rhythm of my heart beats
for my position in the world still reeks.

Someday,

I might come out smelling like flowers,
if only they would give me my flowers
that I might display and nurture to
create a field of my own.

Civility

Civilise me, for I am rough around the edges
that touch and so seep into the fabrics that
weren't meant to be.

Educate me, for I don't understand your
ways, they differ from mine and
I want to know
how you and I might align.

Tell me all that I do not wish to hear and
lend me to the winds that I might be better
in the draft than in the warmth.

I do this to see where love might find me,
alone in a state that pursues me and now I
do not want to run anymore.

A new vision that multiplies my worlds,
meet me on the other side where pastures
green become sour.

I'm no longer afraid of the dark.

Take Me Whole

You were never mine,
so I commit you to the bed first
and then the ground.

Swallow me whole because
the separation of my soul is painful
and messy like the apron of the butcher
who hangs me on display for all to see.
a piece for show,
still, they try to separate me from me.

They stop and stare with interest,
poke and prod with questions about
how I got here,
because somehow
this makes them more ethical and cultured
but it's an intrusion
and one without cause
and still without surprise.

Don't cut me

But on the chopping block I go,
with a few swift hacks of the blade
I am again here for all to see,
but this time taken away
in a nice little package
to be put on ice,
indefinitely.

For MJ

In your passing, we pass together
A little of me leaves with you
The shape of me is nothing without you
The sound of your laugh
The feel of your touch
The smell of your fragrance
The playfulness of your voice
I wish I had made the trip
I really wanted you to see the woman I was
becoming
When I cried, you came
When the lump in my throat appeared, you
rubbed my back,
          held my hand and told me it would
be ok.
The warmth of your home
A place where the madness did not exist
Just the calm I needed

Concrete Tears

I look outside for a glimmer of hope
but I am met with the grey of the skies that
permeate into a network of buildings that
house a network of families who become like
kin but have nothing in common bar the
tears that they cry at night
into the flat pillows they sleep on as they
pray to the Gods on bended knee and with
clenched fists wondering why they are caged
by a concrete monster.

A monster that only ever had dreams of
giving them a better life
and now a symbol of disaster
labelled a sink hole
the concrete cries too.

Absorbing the worries of those it was sworn
to shelter from the elements
until those that did not understand their way
of life demanded for a change,

that it changed its outlook on life and
how it showed up in the world with a new
outfit,
an outfit that was set to appease those who
imposed themselves in the space.

A change of outfit that was sure to be talk of
the town and that it was indeed,
the talk of the town and then nationally as
that outfit set ablaze and those prayers were
never to be heard again.

Now here sits an empty shell of a marriage
between
unwilling participants, presided over by
those who
imposed and enforced a desire that was not
shared by all.

An Avoidance of Pain

In thinking about what it is to be in pain,
I reconcile with the fact that
both pain and grief sit hand in hand
on a wall with foundations so loose that
even the thought of sitting on it
in a moment of weariness provides the
possibility of imminent disaster.

As they attempt to sit,
they fall headfirst.
Who saw it coming and at what pace?
There is a slowing of time that occurs
when we watch one fall,
followed by the seemingly high impact

       smack

as they land on the ground,
lifeless.

It all happened so fast…I ask,
who granted the permit,

who was the architect?

A passer-by whispered…
          their union never promised any
safety

Leaning closer in,
I observe they are still holding hands,
pain and grief on the ground.

As strange as it sounds,
this is where they tell me they need to be.

How often do we want to
lean into the pain that we feel?
I suppose this happens rarely
as we are preoccupied with crafting an
escape from the traumas that we collect
like stickers in the bi-weekly magazines
we amassed as kids.

An exercise that serves us temporarily
done without much consideration
beyond that immediate feeling of

relief because the pain is too much to bear
and even the *light touch* pain is
too much.

Waiting for the feeling we avoid is a
sensation unlike any but one we
have come to know

collectively.

Shipping

Like passing ships in the night,
I might miss you through the fog of my
thoughts,
the misspoken words that I offer
and it seems on this occasion,
decline to receive.

Has anyone ever been so giving
to know that it hurts
to see part of you leave
and enter into another.

Our journeys do not match but they
intersect,
there is much pause for the heaviness that is
felt through your absence.

A lesson learned that time does not
synchronise and that although
our twenties are past
together,
I'm five and you're one,

the list gets longer and the order becomes
different.

The feeling of hopelessness
and all that comes with it.

I imagine another year in captivity
after knowing I've come so close
to a version of freedom
that is uncomfortable but necessary.

This version that dangles
right in front of me,
time lost
connection lost

disconnected
disconnected

I can't stand to be disconnected.

I'm looking for something that feels real.

Something that is real.

Waiting to Exhale

I

      can't

            focus

                    with so much going

            on.

                  I simply can't focus.
What a chore it is to look after oneself when
you are so tired that it feels like your brain
may fall out from the top right-hand corner
of your head and onto the desk right in front
of

            you.

Relationship Glitch

In the deepest section of my phone there is
a note.

A note about you and all the reasons why
this can't work,
all the reasons why this relationship feels like
a dial up connection instead fibre broadband.

     You keep dropping out.

The reasons why it feels like my aunties
calling our
landline whilst I surf the internet deep in its
first wave
engrossed in this chatroom but now

                         I'm
                  offline.

You see, there's a glitch,
a glitch in our relationship.
Our values aren't aligned.

This time, I'm dropping out.

In this section of my phone which is locked
by my expression, under the digits of a
memorable
    moment
I come to vent my frustrations.

I wanted to commit these words to paper
but the gentle way in which my Lamy glides
over the grainless Moleskine page feels too
much of a gesture for you.

As I type away my frustrations
your number comes up on my caller ID.

Mid-flow, mid-sentence.

Sorry, I am unavailable.

This is not love, it is rough like the cheap
paper from that other brand and so into the
digital you go.

At the tap of a button
I am able to delete.

Start all over again.

It's over it seems,
it was fun while it lasted.

Non-descript

Communication takes various forms
it is essential, yet optional.

We signal through its use; positionality,
importance, desire.

Cycling relationships
we attempt to peel back the various layers
of those we hold court with.

What of the perceived connections, the
synergies?

We view something of ourselves in another
elements that we hope will sit in
complimentary nature to our own.

How are you?
        Fine

How are you?
        Good

How are you?
        Ok

How are you? How are you? How are you?

We fill our conversations with non-descript
questions, non-descript answers
and wonder why the foundations are
unstable?

In our choice of language
we create barriers to meaningful exchanges
we create cycles of nothingness
            we create chasms which can only be
filled by
fatigue
we create resentment
we make and then undo

values lost
values found.

The cold space of the liminal

boundaries obliterated
a lack of support for the weary

to rest.

Twisted Fantasies

We connected in a way that wasn't quite
clear and was evidently never about me
but always about you, your wants and your
desires.
An overwhelming pressure that turned into
a dark twisted fantasy, stories that you
concocted and cast us as the players,
but no one knew, except for you

                        the writer,
the architect of the perpetual disaster that
scratches at the surface of my reality.

Pit

A bottomless pit you consumed all my
innocence,

      feeding on a fear that grew in your
presence,

filling a void to quell the feeling of being

    alone.

Imagined Realities

This life is one that is not certain, but I am sure that it leads me on an adventure which I shan't forget even as I pass into the next life and meet the next body or the next sleeve. The possibilities of living in eternal favour, the notion of being left not behind but forward always for the living to remember and celebrate you, to be in conversation with you for you never died, you never left the earth. All that happened was you transcended this space, this container, this body and so here you are. A vision of you that is real, tangible, one to be held one to be questioned. I'm communicating with you, we're building a language together a sequence of sounds which become words and movements which become gestures, this is our means of 'getting to know' because the prospect of our stranger-hood is one that, although attractive, is one that creates space for a fear that I am not quite sure I'm ready to lean into just yet. As in, there is a possibility that all those feelings that were fraught are simply the push that was needed to enter a place of discomfort in order to

push beyond the boundaries that were set for
self with influence from externals who
perhaps know best but maybe not. These are
the stories that we tell ourselves in trying
to find our place in the world, the stories
we tell ourselves as we try to piece ourselves
together from the multiplicity of stories that
we meet along the way. The bigger picture
story that no one imagined because
imagining has become cliché and that
which only children or the naïve do. Because
imagination has been beaten to a pulp by the
manmade conditions that we survive under
because that's right, we are indeed surviving
and yet to thrive because we play under the
rules of those that have an agenda which
is different to our own, because we are too
afraid to speak and maybe let out that the
agenda of the ones we despise and look at
with bemusement in how callous they are
is in-fact the same agenda that we have but
were never brave enough to voice it out loud
because the thought of being ostracised is
one step too far beyond the soft bubble of
individuality which may stand us in good
stead as leaders of the now.

The Stanger is easy

Dear stranger
come close to me
for I can't stand
those who are close to me

in the stranger of company
you

                              sit.

Stop Soothing

Wishing you could go back and give yourself
a hug, looking through pictures of a younger
version of you, you recognise the loneliness
in your own eyes.

Can I hold you? Can I hold me? You still
want to be held now.

You still feel lonely.

They expect something of you.

They are waiting for you to say something.

Sometimes, most times, you have nothing to
say.

Can't speak.
Can't soothe.

Won't soothe

        anymore

tired.

Conditions

Empathy understood?

But there is something about hearing this
woman's
experiences that creates a void of
understanding for you.

In processing these experiences, the default
is to look to her for cause,
a conveyor belt of questions

      "what did you do?"
      "what did you say?"

      "what were you wearing?"

And with a screeching
             halt
the conveyor belt is leaking oil, all over the
factory floor. She slips on your questions
because of all your prompting of

      "are you sure?"

There's no free hotline. No win, no fee.

Just conditions that indicate a lack of belief,
stirring up feelings of doubt.

Now she's taken back to that moment when
her world was turned completely upside
down, inside out.

The world no longer exists or operates in the
parameters that she previously received as
gospel.

The world is now filled with hideous lies,
lies that harm,
lies that threaten her very existence.

The type of trauma that is sustained takes a
lifetime of work to heal from.

Be kinder to yourself.

Prayer

Shield me from those that feel my existence to be an irritant which must be exterminated.

Shield me from the violence of the unsolicited voices that grab hold of my throat to enforce that I have no say.

Equip me with the tools to engage with the traumas from my past which I work to learn from and leave behind.

Give me the grace to identify those that do not contribute to my healing.

Protect me from those that do not wish me well.

Protect me from the lies I tell myself.

Replenish my gratitude.
Replenish my soul.

I am grateful to be alive.
I am not here by mistake.

Ase.

Be Still

Your heart beats fast because you have never centred yourself.

The time is now

> be still.

Your palms are sweaty because the thought of holding yourself whilst you held everyone else was alien.

The time is now

> be still.

Your voice quivers because you are scared of all that you might say and that you may truly be heard because even you have never truly heard you. Not even in prayer.

The time is now

> plant your feet
>
> be still.

A Letter for the Lost

Dear Lost,

It's tricky, you're in the same place that I am,
but I can't quite put my finger on it.

We're in the middle of nowhere which is
ironically somewhere. I can't tell if I'm scared
or a little thrilled as this unknowing points
towards discovery.

My imagination runs ragged with the
thought that this state is exactly that,
imagined.

In reality I knew where I was all along, it just
looked different from your perspective.

Desired Freedom

growth

love   freedom

give in
evolve

                    mindset
wants

        educate
self

A Letter for Desire (Never Met)

Dear Desire,

I feel you much more than I see you. A
culmination of my unthinkable thoughts,
pushing at the tip of my pen and the edge of
my lips, you look for a way to escape
and somehow manifest.

I fear for you. I fear that once you leave the
relative safety of my thoughts, the tools and
the collaborators you need will

fall
short.

All Praise To You

Praise be to you that knows my worth
and sees my light
for I have existed in the dark so long
that even the dimmest of the bunch
seemed like a way out.

I sigh with a heaviness that beckons the
sorrow of those in close proximity
as they come to grips with the truth,
that I am not all they thought I to be,
but some of that and something else.

Dependable with a hint of recklessness,
a dam waiting to burst under the pressure of
the waters that flood through
with an anguish that escapes in and through
all the gaps,
a space deep within.

The fear that sweeps over
like the gentle waves of the sea
become harder and faster,

knowing I am visible for everyone to see.

But how might I escape the expectations
and just be,

make the mistakes I was due
without the need to owe you
for the experience of failing,
simply failing but loving it.

Loving it because it shatters the image
that they knew
and the image that I know,
I thought I knew,
a creation bestowed upon me,
a multiplicity of authors without credit,
living rent free
destroying the interior with no promise of a
return on this security deposit.

House me in a state of homelessness
that I might feel at peace
in a certain place that exists with no base.

A line of uncertainty
in a near sure page that is still being

written.

Becoming

I love the woman that I am becoming
because I saw her from a distance
but could never quite keep up with her.

It was the way she moved
but now we're at a junction,
the point at which we crossover and meet,
a point where we slow down to stare each
other in the eyes,
looking deeply for a sign of recognition,
that I see you and you see me.

A sign that lets me know you accept where
I'm coming from
and simply stand here with open arms to
signal me to the next point along a journey
of redemption
that veers in a cove of acceptance and back
out along a winding road of growth that
occasionally swerved into a nook of anxiety
that grabs me by a
        hook

chew me up, spit me back out
and now I'm on the road again,
peddling through grief and
skating on happiness with high hopes to be
carried and cloaked by

a joy

that I may identify as mine and mine alone
because

that is what it feels like to be at this place,

that she may be finally letting go and
releasing all that does not belong to her
and simply back to those that mask their
intentions and their love
because it has fallen
and here we are,
no more facade,
no more scratching the surface without
getting into the dermis,
you are under my skin
and I understand it now that

under the skin is a privilege,

a place of love
a place of wanting

sitting in between a space of perfect abilities
and meaningless chatter that does not know
how to take all of me.

A realisation that even though my desire is
for you to take me whole
it may never come to pass
because
I reckon with my own flaws
in that I
cannot handle all of you.

So I return to me,

I return to loving the multiple versions of I
that sit under the roof of a picture house that
projects and plays out the scenes of an
internal writers' club who laugh around a
table, who laugh with heart

for this live action moment has
evolved into a script-less play that gives
them space to pause and reflect.

They say,
she loves the woman she's becoming,
flaws and all,
she loves the woman she's becoming,

and I love me too.

Classroom Et Al.

Your magic knowns no bounds. In this, I
cannot be sure if you are one or of the many,
the physical or the imagined - a foundation
for my thoughts.

Either way, it is your invitation to discover
that activates one of many fires within me.

We move from one to another, we pause and
then continue with a dialogue which snakes
around and maybe eats its own tail.

This is my hunger for you, of which,

I will never be full.

Touching Thoughts

It is in your words that I get lost,
the author I do not know physically but we
meet intellectually.

You provide a landscape for me to wrestle on
stretching my imagination and challenging
the constructs of the world that has been
built in part for me and recently by me,
with me.

You guide my curiosity into spaces that I
thought taboo and that I had no say in,
into spaces that don't quite fit with the status
quo and I need it.

I need not to be surrounded by the sweet
sounding yes and must balance that with the
uncomfortable space of tbc, because all of
this is new to me and I'm currently
fingering through the pages that guide me to
this point of thoughts that scream gently to
be let out.

The sensuous sonic qualities of the narrator
who tells this story, who tells the facts?

I'm all ears

and I know that your pen itches
wishing to write the wrongs that we were
denied experiencing.

Wrap me up, write all over me until we run
out of thoughts.

Certainly Warm

Sunlight.

You brighten up my day because the dark is
where I reside,
where I sleep
and I love how you tickle the small of my
back even in the crisp spring mornings.

How you come through the leather of my
jacket, sitting gently upon my skin.

Your touch reminds me of a time without
stress and that I too may enjoy the soft
unfurling thoughts that bring me to now.

I love the way you gently pulsate through my
window
and how I then start to wonder if your
absence might be permanent
for the whole that I feel when you're gone is
palpable.

I run

I run far through the thoughts of summers
past and winters now,
wishing for an exchange because we sit on
opposite sides of a meteoritical year,
we sit wondering what our lives will be
and if the destitution we prayed we would
never see is almost upon us,
because all that we thought,
believed to be promised is in fact
not.

So now we sit here staring at each other
waiting for a sign that we might resume and
get back to normal,
whatever that was.

The sound of uncertainty rings loud in my
ears.

When my alarm goes off in the morning it
isn't a gentle waking tone
but the sounds of uncertainty in not

knowing what the next minute, hour or day
holds.

And so maybe in the uncertainty we can be
sure of one thing,
that we never know and as such, this is our
constant
that we dance through bitter pastures that
might be a bit greener, or become yellower
like the sun that I crave for
because now I don't know,
but somehow it feels better to not have you
occupying the bowels of my heart.

It wasn't fair and I knew and so now I'm
here.

Sitting by the window while the sun coats
my fingers ever so gently,
the warmth of your rays reminding me that
things may get better
and that this life is uncertain.

Observer

Once again, I am in the place of observer,
it is a place that I like, a place that I enjoy,
but when will the observer become the doer?

Quiet and humble, no one notices the
observer because that is my job, I sit here
and watch, looking for the cause in your
actions just in case I can come in as the cure.

Loving Black

I see examples of you everywhere I look,
I just want to be a part of your world,
you are my world.

Black love,
your cause has become an aesthetic,
something they hope will be trend driven
hashtag ridden.

Filter
through a lens
that has no substance and thus ruins a
childhood that is yet to arrive.

Save yourself,
Black love as an aesthetic rather than an
action.

To love each day
while Black is…

Rainbows

Calmly I wait for the love that I am due

  a lifetime of hurt tells me that this

state cannot exist for much longer

  that my rainbow arrived and from

here on out I shall follow the beautiful light

show

  to be guided along a journey that is

always filled with gold.

  The pitter patter of the rain that hits

the ground, the subtle nature of the sun

  as the two become one.

The Winds

Dancing in the winds that hold me sweetly,
I wonder if and when it may stop.

How the rhythm carries you and you carry
me, a dream of two bodies entangled
in a reckless rhythm that takes no prisoners.

I am all yours,
and for a second,
I wonder if you are truly mine,
here in this moment with me.

Your breath against the back of my neck
pulls me out from the deep insecurities
of not knowing my place with you.

The feel of your arms around me
as we continue to dance to a rhythm
that is slightly offbeat but on the point of
our toes and the swing our hips.

And then there are those things,

your lips,
the softness of them and my anxiety of
swallowing them whole.

I can't get enough.

We danced these nights
under the pretence that
dance was dead
and that it was just you and I
who moved
when in-fact it was something else,
the unseen but the present.

The movements of one-hundred men before
you and one-hundred women before me.

All of them each taking place
and directing the next step in telling us
where we might go,
right,
but then left and our hips continued to
move.

They exuded a pride
as a version of them took centre stage
living on in plain sight
in circumstances that were never to be
understood by those that didn't believe that
they existed in a way that was human
and beyond the spiritual
they live through and with us.

As the night winds down
they one by one retreat
to a place that moves forward
to go beyond the distant echo of
an unrecognised voice
which felt familiar and far.

Between

I wonder what may be for you and I?

We exist in realms of unmatched envy and
unparalleled miscommunications.

Where should I be and what should I do?
I sometimes turn to you for answers
but realise that it is I that is mute,
so perhaps I never asked in the first place
which means that there is no answer
which is truly due.

I see the highway of hopes
and the one-way systems that prevent its
free-flowing nature.

The colour of fear that exudes a rough hope
and that refuses to follow any of the rules
just in case it makes sense
and we have to face the realities of where it
is that we exist.

I know that the voice is a gift
but that it could also be a curse
in that the voice giveth life yet it taketh too.

The commands that we might follow
and the difficulty in surrendering
because the thought of surrender echoes
the hallowed laughter that tells us
you are weak and the weakness is
that which I refuse for I am complex.

I am soft and I am hard.
Forgiving and a holder of malice.

Living in the space of grey is an experience
of immense discomfort
because I know that the hues and the shades
are all possible
but just that they are on the other side of
where it is that I exist.

My existence is littered with the
disappointment of the almost there's and the
could-have-beens,

oh how I wish
sometimes we didn't have the in between.

Because maybe what we all truly crave is
the extremity,
what lives on the far and hard end of the
world of our experiences
and how we might feel safe and secure
because it is an absolute
and we can believe it to be true
because our dreams are not always
what we make them
but an infiltration of elements that harm us
and do not serve us

but we give over space
because we do not know any better
and we are told that a place of balance
is where we must exist
and it is best for us,
but when did what was best for me become
an issue or a matter of us?

I just need to know,

not for you but for me,
or is it for the multiple versions of me?

Into the Night Sky

Heavy are my eyes
because this night that has passed,
did not do so gently
and so, felt more like a drag.

I wrestled with sleep,
pleading for the moment
I might shut my eyes
and drift into a place
that I may recuperate from
the affairs of the day,
previous past
but each time my eyes closed
they opened back wide with thoughts.

Thoughts of you,
thoughts of them
an uncomfortable presence that chased me
through the realm of supposed dreams.

Tossing and turning

I listened out for the sound
that might soothe,
a sound of comfort,
a sound of home,
because home is where the heart is
and my heart beats fast
and this is how I remember that
I am alive.

Never mind the anxieties
that keep me up.
I am alive,
but I'm tired.
I lack the energy to say something
which might be beautiful
because my brain is clouded,
                              like that of
                fog.

It's dirty,
but it's not its fault
it is stained by its environment,
and I tried to leave,
I promise I did,

but the boarders were closed and death was
on my doorstep.

A prisoner to a home that should have been
celebrated.
four walls that became my place of
resentment rather than to remain a place of
sanctuary.

I stare at the ceiling,
hoping for it to cave in
and to be exposed to the outside air,
that I might lay with the clouds
in a bed of familiarity,
a bed that harbours my hopes and my
dreams,
a bed that absorbs that sweat of my
excitement and the tears of my sorrow,
laying in honesty,
it never occurred to me that I lay
in this complexity of
want and absence,
divinity and obsolescence.

Building

I am in the habit of building.

I build to survive.
I build to protect.
I build to uplift.

Each day I wake up, I step into a
construction site which is fully staffed but to
my surprise,

I am the only one who is working.

I build not walls nor shields
but this time a looking device so that I can
be seen.

See me in my fullness,
not halves, but whole.

I am complete.

A Thought for Grace

Here is a thought for grace and the ways in which we receive it. A thought for how gratitude is a state of being as opposed to the act of doing.

This morning I am grateful. I am grateful for me and grateful for you because here lies an opportunity to pause before returning to the dizzying speeds of life.

The slow once scared me but now I see its value. Here in this moment, here in bed. The place where I somehow seem to think clearest.

And so a reminder that you are in an abundant partnership with the past, present and your future for the present offers the encouragement we so needed in revisiting wounds past. Like those ripped school trousers, I am finally stitching these wounds.

The Moment is Now

And so it begins, my eyes are wide open.
I see the future that I want and know is
possible
       it is time for me to let go and
       graciously accept all that this world
wants for me.

All that I want for me.

The days spent dreaming and the nights
spent planning, all for this point right now
that I start the doing.

The moment that I start living in the
excellence that I exude because I exist
outside of the ordinary and

                you know this

    too.

A Letter for seekers of Freedom

Dear Freedom,

I understand that you are tired for many of
us feign to know you. There is a confusion in
defining our relationship, where do we start
as I am fearful of the end.

I stand here, with you, hand in hand,
wrapped loosely in an embrace that slowly
elevates me. The melody that accompanies
our coming together is inaudible to others,
it is not for them, but for you and I.

Words without boundaries

                    we

put   these

words to paper
                        in hopes   that

they will be remembered

                        with expectations

that all

                we have shared

wont be lost

you

will   write

the detailed

accounts of their

histories

with

all that   is

performed in the open

and behind closed doors

About the author

Péjú Oshin is a British-Nigerian curator, writer and educator born and working in South London. Her work explores liminality in culture, identity, the built environment and broader explorations of space making through working with artists, archives and cultural artefacts to create and further explore the possibilities of shared experiences across a global African diaspora. Péjú studied Architecture and Design as an Undergraduate, has completed a PgCert in Academic Practice in Art, Design & Communication at University of the Arts London and is currently completing her MA. Her writing and poetic responses have been published both in print and online.

www.ingramcontent.com/pod-product-compliance
Lightning Source LLC
Chambersburg PA
CBHW021331060726

47591CB00006B/1974